HEART OF
BEING

HEART OF BEING

Earth Is a Heart of Being

Kamakaokalani Lightness, M.S.

iUniverse, Inc.
Bloomington

Heart of Being
Earth Is a Heart of Being

iUniverse books may be ordered through booksellers or by contacting:

iUniverse
1663 Liberty Drive
Bloomington, IN 47403
www.iuniverse.com
1-800-Authors (1-800-288-4677)

Because of the dynamic nature of the Internet, any web addresses or links contained in this book may have changed since publication and may no longer be valid. The views expressed in this work are solely those of the author and do not necessarily reflect the views of the publisher, and the publisher hereby disclaims any responsibility for them.

Any people depicted in stock imagery provided by Thinkstock are models, and such images are being used for illustrative purposes only.
Certain stock imagery © Thinkstock.

ISBN: 978-1-4759-3818-0 (sc)
ISBN: 978-1-4759-3820-3 (hc)
ISBN: 978-1-4759-3819-7 (ebk)

Library of Congress Control Number: 2012912880

Printed in the United States of America

iUniverse rev. date: 08/03/2012

CONTENTS

"I" AM THE "I"

ACKNOWEDGEMENTS

KA I

MORRNAH NALAMAKU SIMEONA, FOUNDER

THE FOUNDATION OF I, INC. FREEDOM OF THE COSMOS

THE FOUNDATION OF I, INC. FREEDOM OF THE COSMOS

IZI LLC

Kamakaokalani Lightness, M.S.

LADY OF FREEDOM, AUMAKUA OF THE COSMOS

OUR LADY OF PORTLANDIA, AUMAKUA OF OREGON

PLEIADES, INC.

ABOUT THE AUTHOR

Kamakaokalani Lightness, M.S. is a graduate of MU, Monmouth University in Monmouth County, New Jersey. The author born and raised in Bergen and Monmouth counties began her travels early through several trips to San Diego, California where her father was stationed in the U.S. Navy. Kamakaokalani completed her Peace Corps experience in Tanzania, East Africa and was employed with the New Jersey Dept. of Vocational Rehabilitation in Red Bank, NJ. She married and due to her husband's tour of duty with the U.S. Army lived in Okinawa, Japan for several years. She continued her work in public schools, after her return to New Jersey as a school counselor. In 1976, she moved to Honolulu, Hawaii where she was employed as a Director of a Career Information Center with the University of Hawaii. Kamakaokalani attended a workshop at Windward Community College on Oahu, that same year and met a Hawaiian Kahuna Morrnah Nalamaku Simeona, named one of Hawaii's living Treasures.

The author began meditating while living in Hawaii and found her clairvoyance was triggered through this experience. She felt very at home in Hawaii and became involved with Hawaiiana. Her first meeting with Morrnah in April 1976 was life changing. Morrnah at that time was working with the first crew of the Hoku le'a, as they were preparing for their first voyage to Tahiti. While meditating during that first meeting, with Morrnah, Loyal Garner, a Hawaiian Musician and singer, and the parents of a special child that was later born in August, 1976, Kamakaokalani recognized a piece of jewelry worn by Malia Mossman. Malia had acquired it through her great Aunt who was best friends with Princess Ka i'ulani. Kamakaokalani informed Morrnah that this was to be on the mast of the Hoku le'a. It appears this jewel, which later disappeared, was owned by Lemurian Kings and Queens and represented the face of God and the sacred flame of creation. Loyal was a former Lemurian Queen, and recognized the jewel. Morrnah mentioned that the mother was carrying a child, who was the reincarnation of King Kamehameha. Morrnah also mentioned to Kamakokalani, that she, Kamakaokalani was given the Sacred Cloak of Creation at that time.

After this meeting, Kamakaokalani found herself spending time with Morrnah. They travelled to many sites in Hawaii, while Morrnah was working with her clients. Kamakokalani continued to meditate and it was during this time that the Peace of I prayer came to her. Morrnah informed her that this prayer would one day be said throughout the world. In 1978, Morrnah began teaching the Self-Identity through Ho'oponopono in Hawaii.

Kamakaokalani was authorized through Morrnah to begin teaching classes in Honolulu, and later in Los Angeles. From 1980-1986, Kamakokalani and Morrnah travelled extensively throughout the United States and Canada conducting the classes. It was during this time that Morrnah was inspired to refurbish the Statue of the Lady of Freedom. She thanked Kamakaokalani for bringing this great being of Light out. In 2009, the Statue of the Lady of Freedom was moved from the Russell Rotunda into the Capitol Visitor Center in Washington, D.C.

The Author was in Los Angeles conducting the classes, when she began writing. She completed a screenplay and short stories. She returned to New Jersey in the mid-nineties and continued to write and completed

Planet of the Crystals, in 2007. In 2010 she revised the Novel, and in 2012, "The New Universe", was published.

Kamakaokalani retired from school counseling in 2010 and continues to write from her home in New Jersey, overlooking the Atlantic Ocean.

MY HEART BEATS

MY HEART KNOW IT'S OWN VOICE,

IT SAYS A THOUSAND TIMES A DAY

I LOVE YOU, I LOVE YOU, I LOVE YOU.

MY PULSE POUNDS THROUGH EACH VESSEL,

IT ROARS LIKE A WATERFALL THROUGH
EACH MOLECULE

AND THEN SLOWLY DRIPS IT'S LIQUID LOVE

Kamakaokalani Lightness, M.S.

INTO THE CHAMBER OF MY HEART.

MY HEART OPENS LIKE A WATER LILY

AND EMBRACES THE SUN LIGHT, GOD LIGHT

WITHIN AND WITHOUT SELF.

I EMERGE AND BEGIN A NEW DAY.

OUR LADY OF PORTLANDIA OF OREGON

(©) RAY KASKEY, 1985

OUR LADY OF PORTLANDIA OF OREGON

(©) RAY KASKEY, 1985

POEM ON THE LADY OF PORTLANDIA PLAQUE

SHE KNEELS DOWN

AND FROM THE QUIETNESS

OF COPPER

REACHES OUT.

WE TAKE THAT STILLNESS

Kamakaokalani Lightness, M.S.

INTO OURSELVES

AND SOMEWHERE

DEEP IN THE EARTH

OUR BREATH

BECOMES HER CITY

IF SHE COULD SPEAK

THIS IS WHAT

SHE WOULD SAY:

FOLLOW THAT BREATH,

HOME IS THE JOURNEY WE MAKE

THIS IS HOW THE WORLD

KNOWS WHO WE ARE.

(c) Ronald Talney, 1985

LADY OF FREEDOM, WASHINGTON, D.C.

MORRNAH SIMEONA
SPEECH

In 1989, Morrnah spoke in the introduction of her Bill to the Hawaiian House Committee on Intergovernmental Relations and International Affairs, asking that the Lady of Freedom be recognized as a symbol of WORLD PEACE.

"SHE represents Freedom for the United States of America and for the Cosmos, not just for mankind but also for all of creation. To initiate awakening in the people of our great country is Divine destiny to bring Peace and Freedom to the world and the entire Cosmos which is reflected in the inscription at the base of the Lady of Freedom, "E Pluribus Unum, out of many ONE".

SUNRISE

THE SUNRISE-SPIRIT OF THE GULF OF MEXICO

THE HIBISCUS FLOWER,

HAWAII'S STATE FLOWER

THE BRIDGE, CANADA-USA

MORRNAH NALAMAKU SIMEONA-SUN OF

SUNS, HAWAII'S LIVING TREASURE

INTRODUCTION

Many changes have occurred since writing the first book. We have gone through several stellar systems and continue to accelerate. This acceleration is happening on every level of creation, even to the smallest crustacean.

The atoms and molecules of creation are changing even as we vibrate to a higher and higher intensity level. Our bodies are becoming lighter and lighter. What will emerge is more love of self and others.

A note of discord can make us very ill, due to the intensity of light from the sun and our inner being. So, let us now move forward and ahead into a new dimension of ever expanding energy.

CHAPTER ONE

THE RETURN

Approximately one to five thousand very advanced souls have incarnated to Planet Earth at this time. They have chosen humbly to serve humanity through their earthly incarnations.

We can find them only through their kind acts towards themselves and others. By be-ing totally purposeful in fulfilling God's Divine Plan at this time.

They all know who they are.

SNOWFLAKES, DIAMONDS FROM HEAVEN

EARTH IS A HEART. When we remove the H from Earth and place it in front, we see Earth as a Heart, which it truly is.

Let us look at snowflakes. Every snowflake is a crystal sphere from the SUN OF SUNS. It is being embedded in the Earth, giving unceaselessly of its light and love of the planet. It is God's love for all of us. Like Diamonds from Heaven to Earth.

It has the music of the spheres and the NEW CREATION within itself. Each snowflake is different, totally unique.

All of life is in a snowflake. Snowflakes make no noise, for they are at peace.

It is the Peace of Heaven coming to Earth and melting into the crust of this planet.

It gives life to new plants, trees, flowers and creatures. Earth is constantly growing, never diminishing itself. It continues with great love and care for those here now.

For this is becoming A NEW PLANET OF CREATION.

TURTLES RHYTHM OF THE SEAS

Turtles are very unique creatures of the sea. They have patterns of creation on their backs. Turtles assist in moving the rhythm and patterns of creation while swimming. They move the rhythm of the waves, so as the waves move, so do the stars in the heavens.

The green turtles are among the oldest beings on the planet. They are the BIRDS OF THE SEA and act as compasses for other creatures of the depths. They are the wise ones and ground the energy of the fish, which are like leaves in the waters.

The turtles are like sails for all and act as gyroscopes for many, including the land formations. Within the turtles are all of the history of whatever area they are drawn to. We might consider them the librarians of the sea.

Sea otters are wonderful creatures and assist in the alignment of the star meridians. It is purposeful for them to lay on their backs, as they connect with stars in this manner. Monterey, California is preserving a way of life, which is important to the Coastline.

Whales also assist in holding the land formations intact. Whales are the great sages of the sea and are to be respected as such. As they travel throughout the seas, they hold land formations intact. It is one of their purposes and very important.

CHAPTER TWO

OVER THE RAINBOW

We all know the song, so what is over the rainbow? Rainbow colors are the sacred colors of creation. They permeate through all time and space. The colors are in every atom and molecule of this and every universe. There are many universes.

With the different templates of creation, the song, "Over the Rainbow" explains a lot.

Kamakaokalani Lightness, M.S.

In the opening of the song, "When all the world is a hopeless jumble and raindrops tumble all around, Heaven opens a magic lane". Every thought we think creates a sound within us, propelling us forward. We can create a jumble or RAINBOW PATHS OF LIGHT.

These rainbow paths of light create healing energy within and without, our time and space. Our thought forms create a life of bliss. It is as if we become the rainbow itself and move ourselves into a magical place. This place is a new creation of be-ing.

Music is one of the highest art forms and the sound goes into the highest realms.

We can then hear those celestial choirs or music of the spheres.

On Sanibel Island in Florida there is a Shell Museum. The shells create music, which are the sounds of the oceans and waves. In walking on the beaches, which are covered with shells, are the sounds of the shells. The shells draw to themselves the dolphins and fish at play in the waters. The solar energy fills the seas and lights from the waves dance like diamonds in the drops of water. The sound emanating from the water is "Somewhere over the rainbow".

Important to create loving sounds for yourself first and see where you are guided to be.

IT IS IN BE-ING FIRST AND DO-ING SECOND. Then we are, "Over the Rainbow."

EARTH IS A TIME MACHINE

Universes evolve in a circular orbit. As they rotate, their energy spirals and when it is purposeful, they merge with other universes and become even larger. At a certain time, the universes go into the SUN OF SUNS. Those star formations will have fullfilled their purpose.

It is the destiny for earth to merge with other planets and star systems, within and without a galactic force field. All of it is energy from the SUN OF SUNS.

We are, as is our Planet, a time machine. It is built in, at the precise moment of our creation. Each of us has a DIVINE purpose for being and have chosen before birth to come to earth at a particular time and period. When we fulfill our DIVINE PURPOSE, we can then move forward in our evolvement. So too, do planets, stars, galaxies, and universes. As does Creation itself. We are moving into a new Creation.

The world as we know it is disappearing and will be formulated into a new pattern. as we cross paths with

Divinity. The complexity of Creation would baffle even the most brilliant of minds or super computer.

SACRED PLACES

Certain places, as many are aware of, hold great reservoirs of energy. The four corners is one of them, in the Western United States. It is a rainbow bridge to eternity. It is a magnetic pole, which creates cylindrical energy, which surrounds our planet and holds the poles together. There exists a gyroscope underneath that site, which has been repaired.

Aspen, Colorado is another special place. Those that reside in that area, have a direct connection with all of the rainforests of the earth and other universes. We have within the earth itself, beings of light which reside there and hold most dear the sacredness of this plane of creation. They work continuously to maintain the balance and work telepathically with chosen stewards of the Earth who reside on top. In this manner flora and fauna work in a conjunctive capacity in new creations.

STARLIGHT, Mt. Hood, is the most sacred mountain in all of the Cascades, and is the eternal home of Our Lady of Portlandia, the Aumakua of Oregon. Our Lady of Portlandia emerged from there centuries and centuries ago to foster the growth of the Pacific Northwest. STARLIGHT is one of the Cascades that creates stars and stars and stars, especially for Canada. Canada is the home of the Aurora Borealis.

The Borealis was originally created by Madame Pele to bring together the different dimensions of creation. Within the Aurora is a universal time clock. This time clock is tuned to Divinity's time, no other. As the Time Clock chimes, it moves the various universes, suns, moons and stars.

Within the Borealis is a dimension of Eternity. This is the reason Indians of both the United States and Canada have gravitated to the Aurora. It is also a place where souls enter and exit this plane.

Eternity itself is an actual place in the Heavens, where souls reside who have ascended to that plateau.

CHAPTER THREE

NEW SOULS AND PARENTHOOD

New souls are coming in assisted by beings of Light from the NEW CRYSTAL UNIVERSE, which has been created near the SUN OF SUNS. These new souls have pure hearts and minds ready to serve humanity and the NEW COSMOS. They have never been on earth before. However, each has been chosen for a DIVINE PURPOSE, and is joyous to be here at just this special moment of creation.

It is a loving act of creation for parents, fathers and mothers, and their entire families to welcome them. These souls are karma free. They will greatly expand the light and energy of their families, communities, and planet. These are the great millennium souls that we have all been waiting for. They are being born all around the globe.

In the ancient Hawaiian culture, certain souls were chosen to welcome the birthing of a child. It was very important for a child to be received and welcomed as they came in. A pregnant mother was to reside in a special place for months before the birth of her child and special foods were prepared for her and the child in the womb.

All preparations to create a most loving pregnancy and birthing were put in place. There is a birthing rock, which looks like a cradle on the island of Oahu. It still exists.

Native Americans also have similar places, as do other cultures. Some cultures have forgotten how important it is to be parents. Heaven considers parenthood the highest vocation for a man or woman.

NEW INVENTIONS

This planet is flexing constantly. This requires constant recalibration of the density of matter. As we are all composed of matter (mother energy), we are constantly being adjusted to new vibrations and frequencies. This will continue daily, weekly, monthly and so on. It is part of the change taking place.

Due to this change, a new crystal grid system with new magnetic belts placed around the earth, powered by solar energy will come into existence. This will make our lives much easier and most of all more free. Living freely is the ultimate goal.

Our homes will have solar chips embedded in the walls of the solar dome homes. The homes will be lit when the sunlight hits the walls. The energy will collect in solar disks for future use. Solar disk batteries will arc all of the energy to power all machines and vehicles.

These are small round disks, which are portable and can be placed anywhere. Four or five can be placed in a vehicle and attached to an existing battery. They are thin, like an LCD screen and embedded with solar codes. Each solar disk is personalized for an individual owner. It is like having sunlight in a car. The power can last for one year and then would be re-energized or re-cycled.

There will be energy grids in communities that provide free power to all. The transformer is a wheel that moves creating cylindrical energy. Our vehicles will float or hover above the ground due to the new magnetic force. This will greatly assist Mother Earth in lessening the impact on the ground. Our personal flying crafts will also be powered in the same way.

The cost of transporting our selves and goods and services, will be minimal.

Our clothing and shoes will adjust to various temperatures, so that in every season we will be comfortable.

Our material bodies, are being aligned with the new solar light system, so we can absorb more and more light, Our auras will become brighter and brighter. We will become SUN PEOPLE of the NEW UNIVERSE.

CHAPTER FOUR

What is LIGHT?

LIGHT IS INFORMATION. All of the celestial bodies, including Planet Earth house tremendous quantities of LIGHT. This is information from the Divine Creator, and is always available to us. It is just a matter of tuning up and tuning in. Tuning up meaning ascending. Tuning in is be-ing at onement with THE SOURCE. Bringing ourselves into absolute stillness of mind and listen to our heart of hearts. The SOURCE resides in our own Heart. This is the spiritual center of our OWN

UNIVERSE. We do not have to go outside of ourselves for the answer, it is all within the self.

When we do this, all information in the Cosmos is available to us. I mean ALL. When we truly know, who we are, the Light within shines so brightly. We become a SUN, truly a house of GOD.

Our lives change. We begin to see ourselves and others in a different dimension.
A different dimension is in a different time and space. For we are always moving, as you, the reader began this page, you already have moved into a new time and space at this very moment.

Since LIGHT is information, what do you as a LIGHT OF GOD, have to share this time around? Once you know, then it is time for you to fulfill your Divine Purpose for Be-ing.

CHAPTER FIVE

BLUEPRINT

Our blueprint is a single cell of Divine energy. It has within this cell, a Divine Spark of Creation itself. The Divine Cell has our purpose and destiny for this lifetime.

It is important for the parents of that child to be in a prepared state of consciousness at the time of conception. The act of life is not about self-gratification. Remember, life begins at the moment of conception. In this manner, the father, mother and child are aligned with Divinity.

The Blueprint is like God's thumbprint on us. Our DNA is sacred. If all of the souls scheduled to be born, had been birthed throughout the world, our planet would be in a different place of ascension.

Parents are being brought together for the nurturing of these special beings. Parenthood is a sacred trust, between the father, mother and child. A loving family assists greatly in the ascension of all.

Communities exist in the Cosmos, where family life has the highest priority, work is secondary.

THE CENTRAL SUN

The Great, Great, Great Central Sun is Infinity itself. It has no beginning and no ending. It is forever and evermore. It is the plane of creation itself. All souls, once they are incarnated, can pass into Infinity. Once a soul is in this state, they embody all of the wisdom of I Consciousness. It is continuous ascension. Their presence on earth is like a golden light of the Sun. All benefit from their energies.

ECONOMICS

When we are ready, a new monctary system will emerge. This will be totally based upon LIGHT energy. Cards, similar to debit or credit cards, will be infused with LIGHT energy. This will be done just by holding the card and receiving sun energy.

We will have moved from coins and currency as we now have, including those institutions that maintain that form. This will be based upon purity of heart and kindness. There will be no manipulation of money, because the cards would just disappear. The Light Cards would be transmuted. to pure light.

As we would exist at a higher level of consciousness, products created would be most purposeful for all communities involved. Everyone would be involved in those decisions. Individuals, communities and nations would be aware of the higher purpose of all of life. Exchange of products would be done easily.

This is a time of clear and concise commerce. We would have learned from the past that everyone is responsible for his or her own welfare. We will, once again, have learned to govern our thoughts and ourselves.

FREEDOM

EARTH has not known Peace or Freedom. Before we can have peace, we must have freedom.

FREEDOM is a state of BE-ING. As we set ourselves free, so is all of creation set free. As we create our BE-ING FIRST, so is there a priority in the COSMOS.

There is a planet called FREEDOM, which has yet to be discovered. It will appear when Freedom reigns supreme for all of life on this plane.

Imagine a world, where everyone feels at home within himself or herself. Where we no longer yearn or desire for anything outside of ourselves. We experience the totality of ONENESS WITHIN AND THEN EXEMPLIFY that on the OUTER.

Now, what does that feel like? For each person, it will feel different.

Allow yourself FREEDOM, to be all you chose to be.

CHAPTER SIX

NEW SOLAR DIMENSION

The New Universe that we are entering is a NEW
SOLAR DIMENSION, which will move us into an
eternal dimension of prosperity. This will be conscious
reality, based on wisdom, peace and balance.

All of the old paradigms are collapsing. They cannot
adjust themselves to the new light frequency of the
Sun, as it brings us, (Earth), into a new orbit. No longer
will we be slaves of DE-SIRE. DE-SIRE means moving

away from the SIRE or SOURCE. THE SOURCE IS WITHIN SELF.

As earth moves into a new magnetic orbit, our energies will adjust to this vibration and recalibration differently.

As this new Age of Humanism emerges, it will give us a new perspective of ourselves and others. You might say, the LIGHT is recalibrating our being, BE-ING.

DIVINE ORDER IS BE-ING FIRST AND DO-ING SECOND.

CHAPTER SEVEN

THE MAIN CRYSTALS

The main crystals are housed in the Great Central Sun. These crystals calibrate all of the Star Systems in their area. Areas are called quadrants. A quadrant may house a number of universes. They coagulate together to create a spiral. The spirals then send out signals to other universes. This is done through electro-magnetic waves at a very, very high level, which have never been experienced by those on this planet.

THE PLEIADIANS

The Pleiades is just one Star System. However, this one has been housing "the heavens". Which has been involved in earth's growth and development. As earth has been a wayward star for so long, our acceleration at this time is important for our growth as a planet and a binary system of light.

It is moving rapidly, in order for us to make the tremendous shifts between now and 2016.

There will be more change in the coming years then in the history, the entire history of this plane of creation. We must be prepared for intergalactic shifts of continents, etc.

As nations come into the awareness of their place, time itself will shift into moments. The fragmentation of time is healing. When time was created, it caused a rupture in the creative process. A schism was created by many who are living today.

Those who created this schism are healing themselves and so all time will heal. As we move into eternity, it will disappear.

God's thrust of creation will no longer be interfered with, as the CHILDREN OF THE NEW DAWN are here, are coming and will assist others in bringing Peace. God's Peace on Earth at long last.

CHAPTER EIGHT

CHILDREN OF THE NEW DAWN

These special souls have been born and will continue to come. These are very dedicated souls knowing that our TRUE STATE in life is happiness, peace, boundless frivolity, (playfulness). They have great love for themselves, their families and others.

They are here now. Welcome them, as emissaries of Peace and Kindness. Kindness is our natural state. They are filled with LIGHT and are Lighting—up, the New

Universe. These messengers of God bring wonderful energy to Earth at this time.

"Behold, I come with great joy and gladness". It is written in their hearts to bring joy and peace to this plane.

Embedded within each crystal is a miniature sun. A replica of the SUN OF SUNS. Each has a life force all its own. Sand, for example, each grain is a crystal. The quartz sand is of a higher vibration and is found on some beaches, i.e. Siesta Key, Florida. So, in walking on a beach, we are walking on millions of suns. Each crystal on earth emanates light. This is one of the reasons we are attracted to beaches. The seawater of course is also solarized. Being solarized it has the vibration and frequency of healing energy.

Walking and swimming on a clean beach and free of negative energy is equivalent to a good massage and gym workout. The sand cleans our feet and the pressure points in walking energize our meridian systems. The sea air is filled with pure oxygen, ions and ions.

Perhaps this is one of the reasons we gather with our families at beaches. Those cultures like Hawaii became aware of this at an early stage of development. Clean air and water is essential to all forms of life.

Our bodies in good health create sounds. These sounds then emanate out into the universe and attract like vibrations and frequencies. Our thought forms are also creating sounds. Our etheric mind and body are to be kept in Divine Order. When dis-ease is experienced on the physical level, it is already too late. Cleansing one's thought forms is essential to good health and evolvement. Our world is filled with non-essential sound, which creates chaos in the mass mind.

CHAPTER NINE

MOTHER VENUS

VENICE is really Venus. Those founders of those cities in Italy, Florida and California have memories of Venus. Venus is an old star and has given birth to many suns, moons and stars of the past. Those that reside on and in the planet are not seen. When it is time, they will make themselves known. Many of the products we know today have their origin in Venus. Strawberries are hearts of Venus and chocolate also comes from that planet. Venus is about home and hearth, nurturing ourselves in a most delightful way. This Star came into this Solar System to assist Planet Earth, millennia ago. The transit this year was significant, as our Planet is making its own journey, transit into the Sun of Suns.

The journey of this plane has been long and short, for the end is in sight. The time tunnel has been set and we will not veer away from the acceleration that is occurring. Earth's journey is UNPARALLED. "BEHOLD, I MAKE ALL THINGS NEW".

STAR PATHS

Once a star begins on its path, its journey will continue until fulfillment. We are all moving through time and space. We move, depending again on our evolvement.

Our rate of ascension depends upon our evolvement as a soul. So, as we move along our individual star path, so does each Body of Light. Each dimension, each particle of dust moves along on its path. All of life is moving into Divine Order. Chaos is the opposite of Divine Order and is measured in wayward motion. We might compare it to a magnet, drawing to itself our life experiences.

When our own magnetic sphere, aura, is in alignment, all of our atoms and molecules are lined up. This is done through, PEACE OF MIND. Without, PEACE OF MIND, we are in a chaotic state of BE-ING. REMEMBER, we create all that we are experiencing by our thoughts first, actions second. Memories, good or bad, create what we are experiencing. Triggers in our mind happen, without our conscious knowing. However, our sub-conscious, our second brain, is aware of this. Having a loving relationship with our conscious and sub-conscious, aspects of mind is very important to congruity within self.

When all three aspects of mind, super-conscious, conscious and sub-conscious are in alignment with the Source, we have a new life. There is a new light emanating from our BE-ING. We have a TOTALITY of LIGHT in letting go of the Darkness of the past. These past thoughts have dominated this plane of creation. As we let go, not only do we ascend, but all of us ascend. All forms of life ascend.

BE ONE, AS ONE and fulfill your own DIVINE PURPOSE, and begin to swim into the HAPPINESS CIRCLE.

CHAPTER TEN

THE HAPPINESS CIRCLE

The Happiness Circle is a reality. It exists in the heavenly realms of Creation within the Main Crystal of Creation. As the Main Crystal of Creation releases more energy to life, the happier we become. Happiness energizes itself, and greatly assists in our ascendency as a child of God. HAPPINESS ENERGIZES ITSELF.

HAPPINESS is one of the most powerful forces for good throughout the Cosmos and Eternity itself. It is our natural state of BE-ING. We might say, happiness is the Fountain of Youth. The more we play as children play, the more we become at ease.

Become a happiness seeker, create more of this energy within self and family too.

CHAPTER ELEVEN

TOOLS OF CREATION

So what are the tools? Each soul is so very unique. We might say we are all orchestrating a loving sound of the universal creation of GOD'S BE-ING.

As we are BE-ING, so does Creation. BE-ING is creation itself. Our celestial tools from Heaven are our thought forms. Creating loving sounds for ourselves, first and others second. Our destiny is to be divinely fulfilled. When we change, our families change, our communities change, world, universes and the cosmos. We are constantly changing, growing and evolving.

Those souls who nurture themselves in totality are in Divine Order. They have great love for themselves, first and others second. This love is not of the egoism of the past, but in alignment with their purpose and destiny this lifetime.

They all know who they are, as enlightened ones. These souls have encapsulated a LIGHTHOUSE within self. They are the ONES who inherit the NEW UNIVERSE.

"AND THE PEACEMAKERS WILL INHERIT THE EARTH".

THANK GOD

Begin and end each day in thankfulness. Gratitude for BE-ING. It is important to acknowledge how blessed we are. Bless is Bliss. When someone asks, "How are you"? We can say, "I AM BLESSED." In each greeting, we are affirming I AM. I AM GOD, BE-ING. WE ARE ALL OF CREATION BE-ING CREATION.

AND IT IS DONE.

OUR LADY OF PORTLANDIA

(©) RAY KASKEY, 1985

PEACE OF "I"